A Time When You Know a House:

Poems of Detroit

# A Time When You Know a House:

## Poems of Detroit

by

Mary Minock

Cover: The Detroit Fire Department's Curtis Randolph Fireboat,
named after the first African American firefighter to lose his life in
the line of duty in 1977. The Fireboat was commissioned in 1979
and continues to stand ready to fight fires with sprays of river
water. Docked at the foot of 24th Street in Southwest Detroit.

Photo by Dwight Stackhouse

Cover design by Shay Culligan

ISBN: 978-1-952326-71-4

Kelsay Books
502 South 1040 East, A-119
American Fork, Utah, 84003

*For Lara, Michael, Meara, Josie, Alex*

# Acknowledgments

Grateful acknowledgement is extended to the publications in which versions of the following poems appeared:

*Abandon Automobile: Detroit City Poetry* (Wayne State University Press): "Wildflowers of Detroit," "Down by the Boulevard Dock"

*The Driftwood Review* and reprinted in my *The Way-Back Room, A Memoir of a Detroit Childhood* (Bottom Dog Press): "Freighter Horns"

*The Paterson Literary Review:* "Retrospect on the Byzantium Poems of Yeats"

*Water Music: The Great Lakes State Poetry Anthology* (Poetry Society of Michigan): "Odyssey, 1965"

*The Madonna Muse:* "Accidental Education," "What Avon Meant to Us"

*LPA Express:* "Sunday Dinner"

*Three Mile Harbor* and reprinted in *The Witness:* "The Dream of the Suburbs"

*Peninsula Poets:* "No Land at All," "I Can't Stop Loving You," "Advanced Cake Baking"

*MidAmerica:* "If You Loved Me Half as Much as I Love You," "Georgia Plates," "The Time I Took Patsy Walker up to Holy Redeemer"

*The MacGuffin:* "On the Livernois Bus"

*The Lansing Star:* "After the Riot, 1967"

# Contents

# I.

# All Mere Complexities

# Wildflowers of Detroit

Old gap-toothed whiskered one
look at you:
what front can front streets now put on
with these holes that show the alleys?

Close your mouth,
lest these ruins show
your inevitable brick-strewn
wood-rot muffler-twist cement-crack
bent-wheel alimentary progress.

Don't cry, old woman,
we will sing some songs
and in singing them we will remember:

Here was a house
where a man and a woman marked their first time
and children smelled oil cloth
through the coming of the radio
the going of the coal furnace
the cutting of the elm trees

and they sat on porches
late into the night
with streetlights behind
breeze-rocking boughs
to wait for car carriers
to shudder down streets
with canvas draped around their cargos;
and in the morning, they would tell
fish tales of fins and tails
on the newborn models.

Here was a time when the busses ran everywhere,
the library stayed open
the Irish stayed put
the Jews claimed Dexter
the Polish edged their lawns
Blacks found sanctuary from the South—
worked hard, flourished, created
scrubbed their children
dressed up to go downtown
and tried to sing the tunes
together with your older children
who were jealous.

Here was a time when we almost got it right:
when the car radios played at every stoplight
and cutting across the privacy
and separate wanting
were words we all knew how to sing
and sang together.
We bounced at our steering wheels
to the rhythm and the rocking
and gave your name to the music.

And here was the time
when your older children left
forgetting, not speaking,
to hoard the words to the oldest songs
like money
and so in August
we sing you to sleep
without the German lullabies
and with the rappers' radios
that pierce the night.

Old one of troubled sleep
who forgets her history:
you want to gather all your children 'round,
the gone ones the dead ones
the mariachis the gospel singers
and the vanished Delray Gypsies.
When you remember all of them
you will cycle 'round.

When you stop waiting
for the City to come with its mower
to cut the weeds that hide
the scalp patched with trash
that even your strong fingers
cannot scrub clean,

you will wait for Cadillac.
He is maneuvering
the turn from the blue Huron
into the straits of green water.

He is coming this way.
He will land near what will be the Fort,
soon to meet his Huron, Miami, Ottawa
and Chippewa neighbors.

He will hack his way
through these bark-cracking vine-wood lots
to gather the wild raisins
to pick the wildflowers
*cueillir les fleurs sauvages*
to pick the wildflowers of Detroit.

# Freighter Horns, Southwest Detroit

Every country has its beauty.
In Iowa they stare into the irises
of sunflowers.
Here we listen
in the light after dawn
to freighter horns.
We cannot see the river.
The view is blocked
and has been all along.
Yet we cannot imagine
a country where there is no river
and there are no horns.
The logic of sound—
buoyant in belief
beyond the ground—
awakens us to morn:
against the horns
we invent ourselves.
From there we go on.

# Live in Detroit

so you can become a child again,
follow cracks seesawing
down the alley. Step only on cracks.

Stay, so you can talk with ghosts
who tell you what has been forgotten
in redirected streets and boarded-up

barrooms restored as bakeries.
There is always more to remember,
and the city admits you to what is lost.

Dwell in Detroit because you are stubborn,
because you fear leaving
would start a bout of white nostalgia:

store window displays at torn-down Hudson's,
a trip to Boblo Island, a bottle of Vernor's Ginger Ale.
To stay makes you stridently political.

Live in Detroit because it is real—
tear-dimmed cracked alabaster
gleaming with rubble and broken glass,

an old couch abandoned on the last
cobblestone street with railroad-siding tracks
known only to insiders down by the river.

Endure. And earn the right to resent your noisy neighbors
who park their motorcycle in the yard
and rev it up in the tunnel between the houses.

Live in Detroit because someone
must dwell in ruins. Pigeons roost
in the great hall, shed small feathers

that flutter and stick in the dust
underneath the last oak benches
where no one is waiting for a train.

Why live in Detroit? Because living here
has handed you a burden you cannot drop.
It has given you an edge, good for something

that you cannot name, good for something.

# If Detroit Were a Random Encounter of Her Women

they'd meet at the river:
Madame Cadillac,
Aretha Franklin,
and my crazy Mama.

Mama is fishing off the Boulevard Dock
not catching anything but the breeze,
watching the water flow
down toward the factories on Zug Island.

Aretha gets out of a big pink Cadillac
in a snazzy sequined dress with an entourage
of natty-suited, handsome tall Black men,
one who drags a big box camera.

Mama and Aretha nod and smile
and talk about fish and the weather,
and, being river-inspired, almost burst
into their own lovely version of the same song.

Madame Cadillac comes floating down the river
wearing one of those 1701 ruffled satin dresses—
you know the type—impractical
for getting in and out of a canoe.

So she gamely grabs the ladder placed there
in case anybody falls in the river.
She sweeps up onto the concrete, shakes out her skirt
and poses with a sweating pair of *voyageurs* of her own.

Mama, impressed by the dress, tries an awkward curtsy
just as two odd sisters in Roman togas stroll by
talking about ashes from a pipe, a windy day at river's edge—
the Great Fire of 1805, but saying it all in Latin.

Aretha is amused, Madame C is confused,
but Mama gets it right away and introduces herself
with that toothy smile—*I'm Mrs. Rhodes,*
*and you must be the ladies on the City of Detroit Seal?*

*Speramus meliora,* laments the sister on the left,
raising her wrist to her brow to evade
the broken benches, ruined grass and swirling trash,
while the sister on the right leans in

a little toward her sister, lifts her arms
in a stylized gesture, flicks her hand
to scope the background of the scene.
*Resurget cineribus,* she vows.

Mama is dying to explain the sisters
and practice her high school Latin:
*We hope for better days,* she translates.
*Detroit shall rise from its ashes.*

And Madame C follows the sister's arm
to spy Aretha's car in the parking lot:
*I don't know what it's for, this armed voiture,*
*but I see my husband's crest, our name on it.*

Meanwhile, Aretha's camera guy is all set up.
He gestures for the ladies to squeeze
between the toga sisters and freeze for the photo,
lumbering trucks on the bridge upriver as background.

And then Aretha starts to sing,
holding the howling notes so long,
trills and surface ripples like the river,
frosting to the depth,

all the way back to Madame Cadillac
who kept the books, kept the colony alive
while her husband was back in France
pitching it to king and investors,

all the way back to Father Gabriel Richard
who put words of hope into the mouths of sisters
after the fire left only one shed standing
at a time when to be prophetic you spoke in Latin,

all the way to Mama
who knew her history, knew her Latin,
all the way forward to Aretha
who stokes embers in ashes.

# Retrospect on the Byzantium Poems of Yeats

*Astraddle on the dolphin's mire and blood,*
*Spirit after spirit!*
        —William Butler Yeats, "Byzantium"

In the old days
a Catholic girl was taught
to slide off the raft
of her achievement
gracefully
so that even as she drowns
she will not make a splash.

So it was with me
the day I was called
to Professor Schmittroth's office
and told I had won third prize
in the intercollegiate contest
for my essay.

He told me he was baffled
that they'd chosen mine;
as he said, *I thought*
*the men's essays were stronger.*
So I went around to all the men—
John and Dan and Bill and Jim—
and apologized to each.
I told them we couldn't account
for the error of the judges.

Still there was the inexplicable
that couldn't be submerged—
the great Yeats poems, the art
my undergraduate pen had wrought
comparing them with Blake's,
my struggle to do them justice
writing in the middle

of howling winter nights,
my mind private and ablaze.
I trembled in the fire
when I read the holy lines aloud.
I swam in the tide
of their irreducible mystery.

I thought I might buy with the prize money
a collected clothbound Yeats
and a clothbound Blake in celebration,
but on transferring from the Dexter bus
to the Baker bus downtown
I changed my mind.
Instead I bought a blue dress
with white polka dots
and a pretty boat neck
from the Woodward Shop at Hudson's.

I never saved the essay—
it was about immortality and art—
Blake the singing master to Yeats' soul.
I never saved the essay
but I know there was a typo in my essay's title,
a word I'd inadvertently coined—
*etenrity* to mean
*The Artifice of Eternity.*

I still read the poems aloud,
the narratives of humility
the corrections of arrogant assertion
*all mere complexities,*
*the fury and the mire of human veins.*

I read them still,
and in the sleepy kingdom of the Emperor,
I sing along with Yeats.
Through a blue eternal Mediterranean
I cling to and ride a dolphin
who contorts his watery neck
to turn to smile at me.

# Odyssey, April 1965

*To Dan*


I think it was my idea
that winter semester
we were reading Joyce.
*What if we got on a bus*
*and hopped off whenever we felt like it?*
*Then on again*
*until we felt the same?*
*We could ride all over*
*Detroit on transfers.*

We'd see what it meant,
our odyssey,
when it was over.

What of deliberately getting lost
on the Eastside? And finding our way out.
What of Mount Elliott Cemetery
that we discovered for the first time
when we saw the stand of budding trees ahead
and pulled the cord?

Old, quiet, monumental:
we picked our way
among the trees and tombstones—
young lovers hand in hand—
a life ahead, a marriage—
descending into Hades,
strolling on the mounds of the dead.

Later that evening, we ended up at my mother's—
that year I didn't live at home
but out near campus.
I think it was the first time you met her.
She fed us a Sunday dinner

as though she'd had it planned.
You washed dishes at the kitchen sink,
singing, with the window open
to the space between the houses,
the smell of earth
and mild spring air.

# Photograph of a Thirteen-Year-Old Girl

I've always been baffled
at what possessed me, all on my own,
to dress up nice—
the way I thought was nice—
my hair severely pulled into a ponytail,
a nylon scarf to tie it,
a white hand-me-down sweater
that I made believe was new angora
when in fact it had been washed
at the wrong temperature a dozen times
and had become like all my sweaters:
dense and scratchy as a rug.

What possessed me to whiten my face
with powder, smear lipstick
on my protruding lower lip
and walk up Vernor Highway
to that photographer's studio
across from the Stratford Theater

where ancient unclaimed wedding photos
sat dusty in the shop window
along with men in Navy uniforms and their girlfriends,
and angelic babies with traces of tears
in the nervous smiles they made
when someone waved a teddy bear in front of them?

Somehow, I do remember my singular determination:
I was going to do it—perhaps to see if there was any glint
of hope that there was something in that face of mine,
something not irredeemably ugly.

I grabbed my sock of babysitting money,
put on my coat and winter boots,
marched the three blocks up the highway
through the slushy snow
in a cold excursion to face the truth.

And so I entered the studio
of that strange Hungarian man
with the piercing eyes
with no one else around and let him sit me down
in front of the screen
that showed two barren tree trunks—
a black one and a pocked white birch—
with a stand of pine trees farther back
and a sloping meadow even farther back,
and *snap, snap, snap* me with that big box,
that stationary photographer's camera,
with him peaking at me with his florid face
hidden behind its curtains
for what seemed the longest time
until he had me scared and embarrassed,
contemplating an escape route if need be.

The result was impossible to hide—
the contact strips revealed the same girl
in basically the same pose:
a freckled thirteen-year-old girl
of the most remarkable sincerity.

How I despised the finished photo
and that ugly girl,

how I set about to study her,
to camouflage and change her,
learning how to hide my natural lip
while applying lipstick,
learning how to tweeze my eyebrows,
learning to wear bangs
because my forehead and hairline
were much too high.

Now I see that strange photographer,
who said little but stared so sharply,
as an artist molding mystery—
the smile reminiscent
of the *Mona Lisa.*

And how she calls to me now
becoming more a child, a pretty little girl
on the beginning side of pleasing.

# Mrs. Dragon

Mrs. Dragon, an ancient Romanian woman,
owned the house next door.
She wore a pearl pendant on her abundant breast,
made pastries on Halloween
that we threw into our pillowcases and spoiled.

We were just children, had no idea
of the labor and love she put in.
We'd rather have had bubble gum or a Mary Jane.
We worried about dates and raisins and wanted
the candy in wrappers.

Now I understand her better,
her old-world pride, her snow-white hair
that had once been raven.
She used the recipe passed down from her mother.
Her flaky little pies in our pillowcases
were pounded by the apples.

We didn't like the apples either.
We were children after soft things,
all that had texture was like crows baked in pies—
strange, a torment to our tongues
and round little mouths
that pursed, remembering, it seemed,
the time before our weaning.

We were children after stories,
but we couldn't hear her stories—
in a dark language that was hidden.
Even when we saw her smile,
the whiskered lips opening
like petals of a rose,
we didn't know her loneliness
was our loneliness.

# Accidental Education

At the holy store we bought
Titians for three cents each
and traded them for Raphaels and Botticellis.

We gazed at many lesser-known
Italian Renaissance painters
of all the scenes of Our Lord's life—
from his glowing presence in the straw
to the glorious iconic representations,
the Good Shephard and the Sacred Heart.

At home I sat on the dirty gray rug
and arranged the holy cards:
Nativity,
Epiphany,
Flight into Egypt—
all the way up to The Agony in the Garden,
the Crowning of Thorns,
the Bearing of the Cross,
Crucifixion, Resurrection, and Ascension.

Then I arranged those of Mary,
Our Blessed Virgin Mother:
the Annunciation, the Visitation, the Holy Family,
on up to the saddest scene, the Pieta, and then
the Assumption into Heaven.

My heart soared with devotion—
Our Lord, who suffered;
Our Lady, who in all her portraits
could be counted on for beauty
even when she didn't wear blue as she should
but wore a cape of deep brownish red;

the saints, who rolled their eyes toward heaven
and suffered like I should suffer.

I took the stack to the dining room table
where I could see the cards better in the light.
My faith leaped like a joyful fish
clear out of the taken-for-granted water.

On the back of a painting of Our Lord
gazing heavenward with his pale blue eyes
and crown of thorns and two soft tufts
growing out of his slight blond beard,
I composed a prayer in a shaky cursive:

*Dearest Jesus I love you.*
*I know that you love me*
*because you died*
*on the cross for me.*

And then I noticed something else:
some paintings were flat;
but in others there were uncanny things—
you could tell how far
the angel stood in front,
how far the garden
receded into the background.
It seemed a miracle that
even when it wasn't in the picture
I could see the source of light.
It was my first accidental course
in Art Appreciation, in Perspective.

# Sunday Dinner

I cup my hands and lean against the glass
to see the sun slant down

as a thousand starlings land
in the trees at twilight.

They jabber, settling down
across the wide white park

where they rest on stick feet
upon the bare black boughs.

Mama steps out on the porch
to get the paper thrown by the newsboy.

I've seen the trajectory of where
it whooshed and landed silently upon the snow.

The cars crunch by on snow tires,
and behind me Mama whistles over sizzles on the stove.

Our light inside is dim,
but the room and I are reflected in the window.

I cup my hands and lean against another window;
the park is darker, and I think I see a man

disappear behind a tree, disappear into different smells
of pork chops and potatoes on the stove

that drift to the window and are trapped.

# II.

# The Dream of Leaving It

# The House That Holds Its Dead

*Dixon House, Southwest Detroit, 1908*

I.

In the old fruit cellar
beneath this house
built over an older house
the spirit of a runaway waits
through webs for dark,
a guide to tell him
the riverfront is clear,
the boat is waiting.
It is his final stop,
so close to the end of it.
He wraps his hands around a cup.
He dreams of dark, of fortune
across a moonless river.

Whatever his fate—
to make it to Canada,
to learn to be free—
the house has captured him.
He haunts this advantageous dark,
this advantageous place,
a cup and spoon beside a stool,
a forgotten mason jar of peaches;
he is a shade still patiently waiting.


II.

Old Man Dixon plays in a sunbeam
changed into a rainbow in the beveled glass,
his office in an upstairs room.
He bids his secretary to record
the words he thinks have wisdom:

*A life not dedicated*
*to some worthy purpose*
*is like a tree without shade.*
He is an important man;
he writes publicity for the city.

*Detroit*, he dictates and she types,
*is a city of five Ps.*
*We have pride, we have pep, and we have push;*
*all these have taught us*
*progress and prosperity.*
She types, her eyes grow dreamy,
and when she hangs on his every word,
the gentle weight of her is fetching.

He steers his secretary down
down onto a dusty sofa.
He shall have pride and pep and push
again, again for years,
and still they are here,
shades of dust, tumbling
in the jeweled sunbeams.

Old Mrs. Dixon shuts her anger in a downstairs closet;
she baffles the downstairs kitchen,
swells like a cupboard door that will not open,
a drawer that opens skewed
and must be closed again and righted,
a door that must be slammed to close.
She is queen of the downstairs kitchen;
her husband and his paramour can hear her cooking,
smell her pungent stew as they right their clothes
wrap it up for the day
in the room directly above her.

III.

Mama has free rein
even though I finally threw her memories
into a steamer trunk and chucked it
into a remote room of the basement.
She might rather be sitting upstairs in her chair
overlooking the park through voile curtains,
but she cannot live without her things.
She shares her hats with great granddaughters
who learn of her and call her by her name,
her hats, her baubles,
her sample vials of mild perfume,
her rosary beads, her costume jewelry.

She can be called upon to invite you
to the daily life of a banded stack of gas bill receipts
for 1935, all there, always all there,
her fat open handwriting declaring *Pd.*
in intermittent black or blue fountain pen.

She keeps rings of keys to lost locks,
and they are sticky with stories—forgotten blizzards,
unhinged doors, the night
the drunk barreled down Clark Street,
plowed into every parked car.

# Ecstasy on the Litany of the Blessed Virgin Mary

*Holy Redeemer School, Detroit*


What divine poet penned
the litany we would sing-
song in our pews and ponder?
*Holy Mary, pray for us,*
*Holy Mother of God,*
*pray for us.* Oh pray for us, oh say it
over and over again, pray for us,
until the rhythm
of our lungs and larynxes
is a prayer, a dance, a chime,
a rocking: instruments
of music our bodies.

*Holy Virgin of virgins,* our Mother,
our *Mother most pure,*
*Mother most chaste,*
*Mother inviolate,*
*Mother undefiled,*
and we trilled and warbled words
that worked our mouths into melody,
that taught us sound
unbounded by meaning.
Say it over and over: inviolate,
*inviolate, undefiled,*
*Mother most amiable, Mother most admirable,*
Oh Mother, my body is laughing with the sound.

*Virgin most prudent,*
*Virgin most venerable,*
*Virgin most renowned,*
*Virgin most powerful,*
*Virgin most merciful,*
*Virgin most faithful.*

Oh Virgin, oh Virginia, oh Vergil, oh Vesuvius,
Oh *V,* oh letter *V,* oh *V,* oh say it and the lips
move toward the velvet side of gentle.

*Mirror of justice.*
*Seat of wisdom.* Oh how
can Our Lady be a mirror?
How can Our Lady be a seat?
We travel now in a land of magic,
in the middle of the song
in the middle of this ride
our bodies take
on a carousel of verse
so eternally in the middle of the song—
of *Vs,* of vessel, *Vessel of honor,*
*Singular vessel of devotion.*

Oh Mary, thou art a *Mystical rose,*
a *Tower of David,*
a *Tower of ivory.*
Oh, Mary, thou art a rune of hurled phrases,
each more beautiful than the one that came before.

*House of gold,* set near the tower,
the tower of ivory,
in an eternal city
where the *Ark of the covenant,* and the *Gate of heaven*
shine as brightly as the *Morning star.*

*Queen of angels,*
*　　　Pray for us.*
*Queen of patriarchs,*
*　　　Pray for us.*
*Queen of prophets,*
*　　　Pray for us,*

and when we get to Queens
we know the end is coming
slowing down
restraining us, arresting us,
and warning us
the poem and ride will end
to the blinking of our eyes
as we stumble out the side door of the church
into the cold afternoon sun
and sea of concrete on the playground
on the First Tuesday of each month
when all in the world is well.

# Mama's Coats

The first one I nagged her out of—
a carmine-colored soft suede jacket
my father bought her in the days
when she was young and relatively thin.
I was young and thin then, in college
living at home, and the red
brought out some glow in me,
so the rip on the sleeve and the sagging
lining didn't much matter.
Walking home through mounds of fallen leaves
on a blue-sky day,
I loved the raw collar,
the rub and heft of that old jacket.

The next one I wore in my early forties
when I lived in Brooklyn—
a taupe spring coat with simple lines and silver buttons,
elaborate pieced balloon sleeves with piping,
matching silver buttons at the cuffs.
It was already moth-eaten, but I darned
the holes so they hardly showed,
wore it like a second skin, giving, stretching,
surprisingly warm and worn,
down those streets and over to the City,
walking fast, wearing red lipstick.
I wore it until the silk lining was ribbons
and I had to pin it in the back.
I never threw it out. I always think
I'll tailor a new coat from its pattern.

The rest came to me later
when we cleaned the backroom closet
with three stuffed rods of all her clothes.
I gave most everything to Saint Vincent's,
but I kept a few of the stylish dresses
my father had bought her
and most of the coats.

I wear the white wool 1950's crepe
with its full Loretta Young skirt
and perfect large early plastic buttons
for drama. One time I carried it
with all its bulk in a suitcase to Sweden,
wore it in the blue hours of afternoon
after the sun had gone down
on the day of the winter solstice.
White coat, white snow, blue twilight, dark trees,
me, with traces of her smile.

# Sewing

I.

There was something graceful about me then,
at the end of the gauntlet of adolescence—
thin wrists and ankles, long hands and legs,
and freckled arms that seemed to lilt in gesture.

I used to ride busses home from college classes—
maneuvering a trip downtown on transfers
to window shop at Hudson's.

And then one semester I discovered sewing,
working on costumes for the Players,
apprenticed to a woman named Alice
who taught me not to pick up pins
dropped on the dusty floor—
they could spoil a lovely wedding dress
we were making for one of Shakespeare's heroines.

The work of pin and thread,
the joining of cloth consumed me—
a process where at every step
I strove for perfection—
from the laying out of fabric
where I checked and double checked the bias,
sometimes stretching and steaming it true,
folded it perfectly and pinned the fold, then rested,

then pinned the ironed tissue patterns
from designs I'd studied hard—sometimes sitting for hours
at a table with the catalogs on Hudson's fourth floor,
flipping, marking pages, imagining myself
and contemplating all the possibilities
of line and color and fabric and difficulty,

choosing the most perfect fabrics,
a lime green all-cotton calico, the feel and heft expensive,
a crimson of a different calico,
to make another dress from the pattern variation—
one with a yoke and the other Empire.

Then it was all for me, this art, this anticipation,
this uncanny love I felt for my body.


II.

Sewing would stay me through the years
when I broke the seals on latest record albums—
put them on the turntable, returned to laying out and cutting,
marking and threading bobbins.
I would start on the machine
but sometimes stop it long enough to study lyrics,

and then to listen for a baby waking up—
working fast against that time—
learning the measure of that selfishness I could indulge
before I'd hear her stir and go to her—
greet her, pick her up, feel her damp hair clinging to her cheek,
marvel at the intensity of a baby's sleep,
wonder how it was for her, what reassurances she needed,
to her this process of sleeping and waking so unfamiliar.

I loved marking out those episodes.
I sewed to the rhythm of her napping, and then her brother's
napping—
a mother on duty, but with her singular pleasure on the sly.
I used the babies as a deadline; if I were lucky
I could finish a sewing step and put my work away
just before a baby started to cry.

The children grew up with it,
watched *Gunsmoke* and *The Waltons* on TV,
while I sat with them, finishing a seam.
They got used to it—a mother whose fingers were always busy,
a whirl of colors on her lap—wide-waled corduroys and tweeds,
raw silks and organdies, brocades and velvets.

# Shift's End

*Timken Roller Bearing and Axle, Detroit, 1958*

At four o'clock the whistle blows,
and men stream out
from all the gates of Timken's.
They separate themselves
to file in lines
directly to the barrooms
that in those days claimed
each corner of the intersection
of Fort and Clark Streets.

Their faces are gray,
their walk restrains a wish to run,
their eyes are urgent.

From across the wide street
I watch their processions.
They scare me some.
To look at them directly
seems to violate a kind of privacy.
I am just a schoolgirl
waiting for a bus downriver.
But listening to the women
of the neighborhood, I know already
I want to marry
a man who works the day shift.

Their faces are masks;
feelings are hidden,
restraint a common understanding
of the work they've finished for the day:

the wait of it,
the patience,
the song or jingle in the mind's ear
in counterpoint to the pounding,

the eyes that stay put
concentrating on the task,
the legs that stay still
while the arms reach
to take and touch the object
change it perceptibly
then let it pass.

These men strive for dignity
and in it is the guessing game for me:
what would be the way to love one?

In the art museum
high above factory scenes
are women painted on the walls,
round as embryos within embryos.

They are cups, bowls that hold fruit.
They keep secret the hours
when the masks are taken down
and gray faces color
with laughter.

# The Dream of the Suburbs, 1955

In those days
in the neighborhood
was the dream
of leaving it:
escape to the northwest side—
brick houses with working screen doors,
aluminum grills with curlicues
to ban them bellying;
a mailman works the beat
and birds chirp quietly.

The dream of Dearborn—
the streets offer more
than plumbing supplies
and used furniture;
there are dress shops
and diversions—
bowling alleys and miniature golf
a youth center
a little city hall
with a cornice like an A&P
a swimming pool;
the houses are laid out for normal people—
no dark hallways
no steep stairs
no moldy cellars.

A three-bedroom ranch home in Inkster—
a picture window
*all for only nine thousand*
*nine hundred and ninety-nine dollars.*
*And ninety-nine dollars moves you in.*

The bliss of the suburbs—
the reasonability
the shopping plazas
where you can go from store to store
a fat green Cunningham's Drug Store on the corner
bigger than the Cunningham's on Junction
withered and shrunken to hold
the little we have to buy.

No warehouses at the end of the street
no pounding out of tin at Timken's
no smell of tobacco in the early morning
from the Scotten-Dillon plant
no trucks shuddering down the street
no cutting of trees in the park
no closures of swimming pools
for lack of chlorine in polio season.

No migrations of new people
no threat of the poorer moving in
to replace the ones
who got their dream ten miles away
no bums from skid row coming our way
down Vernor Highway.

Oh ranch house
oh three doors to open directly
on three separate bedrooms
oh laps of three bright-colored
wall-to-wall carpets
oh vacuum cleaner of many implements
oh windows that work

oh fenced back yard with disciplined little trees
oh suburb
oh sameness, no peeling paint
no passageways, no junk rooms to hide.

There would be new dresses with price tags
to show to the neighbors;
the women would have time for coffee
the women would talk about sales on lamps
stockpiles of canned goods and Saran Wrap
the women would be wise about colors
the women would have painted nails
the women would use mops and electric mixers
in Loretta Young skirts
instead of hands and knees
in rosebud zippered house dresses
the women would wait for men
who worked in suits and were gone all day
no split shifts
no afternoons
no night shifts
no heavy wrists holding beer cans on the table.
Oh suburb—dinner at six
the man, the newspaper, the boys on shiny bicycles
arrive at once
hungry and civilized and feedable.

The dream of the suburbs:
after they were gone
we were lonely
we kept our time by the seasons
we rose in the morning
we settled in the evening
with the sparrows and the pigeons
and looked to the river.

# No Land at All

Mama had a knack for finding forlorn paintings,
often handed down from others,
to hang on our wobbly walls.

Like the one she said was called *Land's End.*
The painting was of nothing but blue waves
that rock against a gray storm-clouded sky,

heaving waves unsure where to go.
No boats, no birds, no leaping fishes,
no relief in breaking on a shore,

only beckoning, bewitching waves;
the painting should have been entitled
*No Land at All.*

She had another called *The Lone Wolf,*
a brown wolf in profile in the foreground
on a snowy hill on the stillest winter night.

The wolf gazes off to the left
refusing to look down
toward the lights in the windows

of the little village
nestled in the valley
in the background on the right.

The wolf—he is cold.
The town—it is warm.
The message—it is clear: it's the lone wolf's choice.

For him it's fascination with snow
so cold it squeaks like an opening door;
it is the smell of night,
the silence, the freedom of the howl
that will not be burdened by an answer.

# If You Loved Me Half as Much as I Loved You

*Vernor Highway, Detroit, 1962*

I.

Patsy Cline under our skin,
we walk her cadence
past the exhaust fan of the Three J Bar,
smell extinguished Camels and bourbon
from around the corner.

Snow melts fast these days—
factory specks are on the heaps of it
and spring is in the air.
The weatherman calls it high pressure—
the air lifts the water and carries it downriver
over the lake and dumps it
somewhere east of Cleveland.

II.

Patsy sings the words
we will learn until our hearts are seasoned—
half as much would be enough,
and only women somewhere else
in other neighborhoods
with cleaner snow and spaces
between the houses and the factories and the bars
would ask for more.

Mama croons along—
she loves a good tune.
If she knows anything

about this love half-good
she isn't saying.
At least she isn't saying
that it will not do.


III.


We are too young to know
the insides of the lyrics,
the insides of the country
bars on Vernor Highway,
but we are excited
by all the handsome southern men,
red-headed and red-faced,
who pomade their hair into ducks' asses
and wear white wool jackets
cinched at the waist,
tight blue jeans.

Hot blood in a deep front pocket
and a soft leather wallet
in a shallow back—
thick on Friday afternoon,
a curved signature
from riding on their fannies.

We know these are the men you'd die for.


IV.


Patsy under our skin,
we cannot help it:
He opens the door with the diamond window

against the noise of the traffic and the busses,
the heat of this cold northern city.
*Air Conditioned Cool Inside*
drips the sign and it is true.
It all spills out on the highway—
and he drawls at you,
*Hi Sugar. Want to come with me?*
Maybe you would have gone
but you knew no graceful way
to discard the school books
and the groceries.


V.


At the end of the day shift
in the gray afternoon,
Ace sits on a bar stool
in the dark Three J
while Liz waits at home.
She puts a 45 of Patsy on the hi-fi.

Half as much means just enough:
he'll be home for supper
sobered up enough to eat the biscuits,
notice the new gingham shades
on the lamps,
the new tooth popping through
the young one's gum,
the new words heaving up and out
of the mouth of the oldest.

VI.

Friday nights on Vernor:
we pile our hair a mile high
and walk on high-heeled boots.
They ride with the windows down.
In the honky-tonks
they fight or curse or puke
or dance to the bass beat.

On Saturday we start
to start again:
we will have hoped
for half as much by Friday.

# III.

# Odes on Memory

# Letting the Fire Go Out

These days the park is cold,
white beyond the white voile curtains;
the snow tracked on the inside stairway
marks my trail of coming home from school,
that snow and a grainy swirl of it
at the corner of the doorway down below.

My boots that latch like firemen's
with fake-fur borders
lie at the top of the steps,
one sliding one way, one the other.
The cold snow makes no puddles;
it will not melt.
The fire is low.

All my mother asks of me
is to keep the fire going.
I am nine years old, then ten, eleven.
And we are old-fashioned,
the only ones who keep the ritual:
coal truck pulling up,
wheel barrel or conveyer belt,
coal chute,
loud spill,
dark bin,
and curious boys from the neighborhood.
Everyone else has converted to gas.

On the October day the truck arrives,
she goes down to greet them,
loud greetings, public process all around.
I hide. I always hide—

against the heat register in the bathroom.
I pray the winter will be mild,
for if it's not, they'll fill the bin again in February.
And then, on bitter afternoons after school
there is danger of the fire going out.

I've been told how to fix it—
five good shakes
of the handle of the monster furnace,
three shovels full of coal
banked on left or right,
whichever way is opposite
to her way of the morning,

then open the lower door,
shovel out the ashes and the fallen clinkers,
fill the water chamber from the bucket—

all will keep it going;
but it's loud,
and the ones in the flat below
have a furnace converted to gas.

I cannot sneak down the back stairway
past the sounds of the lady in the downstairs kitchen
cooking normal meals, making normal sounds
of cleaning up and pleasing.

I cringe against the heat register,
wishing we had a new furnace,
wishing we had someone else to fix it
and it wasn't me: this girl in training
to obey her mother once.
I am a bad girl; I will press against the ebbing.
I will let the fire go out.

At five thirty she'll be home,
and she'll feel it, even on the stairway:
*Did you fix the furnace?*

*Did you let the fire go out?*

# Lost in Song

Mama was moved
by songs of love in romance languages—
*Vaya con Dios, my darling,* the melody
that sets the path of gone and never more.

And I was a savant of lyrics
and memorized them quickly—
after only one week on *Your Hit Parade.*

Such travel they offered in my mind—
exotic places borne on catchy tunes—
"Hernando's Hideaway" where you
*knock three times and whisper low
that you and I were sent by Joe,*

or Monterey in old Mexico where
*stars and steel guitars
and luscious lips as red as wine
broke somebody's heart,*

or to *a pawn shop on the corner
in Pittsburgh Penn sul vain ee ah.
But I ain't got a thing left to hock.*

And then it didn't seem
like we were only fragments of a family,
just me and Mama gazing
into the little Admiral TV
for we knew all the songs and sang them all.

She taught me beguine and tropical splendor
and harmonized in her clear alto.

She translated the foreign words I didn't know—
*May God go with you, my love.*

# Always . . . Clark Park, the 1950s

### I.

                              In winter,
how the snow crusts after the first day,
how the moon from the southeast rises clean,

casts gold across ice on the lagoon,
climbs scales in our porch window's right edge,

how the herds of birds land hard
in studded black clouds that blanket every tree,

how they squawk and flutter, bicker, hunker down,
become still, become silent, fall into standing sleep.

The wind blows across the park toward our closed windows,
sets curtains waving, each pane rattling in its sash,

radiates an inch or two of cold
to counter the coal furnace blast.

### II.

Always, it takes time for the park to come alive:
dormant dun lawns, dirty lagoon—leaves turned
to bottom muck, surface strafed with broken branches.

Puddles claim the ground of spongy grasses.
You walk in early spring, tiptoe around
or hop over muddy places on the path.

The swings have been taken down for winter.
Air drips, and somewhere down near Fort Street
a factory's dull thumping, dropping.

Always, on a day you are in school,
they reattach the swings
clean and fill the lagoon with fresh water.

You have to stop thinking about swings
in order to be surprised.


III.

                                        On summer nights
we glide slowly back and forth
on the upstairs porch swing—
keep vigil on the night life of the park.

Quiet park, hidden by glare of streetlight,
no sounds or small sounds—crickets,
occasional rustlings, click or groan of an old tree limb,
pressed into fanning by a breeze.

All those leaves, all those trees, all that chlorophyll,
all that night making oxygen—
deep dewy ground-hugging clouds of it
so that after midnight the park turns from cool to cold.

The park gives us what we never have to earn:
alchemy in the secrecy of dark.

IV.

After they build the ice rink down the park,
they stop filling the lagoon with water.

In fall, Western High School ROTC boys
march at the bottom, back and forth and up the side,
belt out military chants while some adult honks orders.

After a ceremony around the flagpole, echoes
of shouts and boots are quelled by taps of a lone bugle.

September is hot. Then leaves from twenty trees
fall into the lagoon, are lifted by wind in batches,
blow in swells toward the east end.

Rains come, by November leaves
are stirred into soup. The first freeze

sees flapping maple leaves pinned in ice—
maple, oak, poplar, all of them,
a crackling tearing random pattern.

# Bad

I was a bad girl. Sister Florita said so.

At least I was quiet,
and so I thought maybe
I might be better than I thought.
After all, I couldn't even imagine
doing what the really bad boys did
at the band concert in the park—

after all the grown-ups in the neighborhood
had seated themselves
and we kids had spread our quilts
on the grass in front at the foot of the bandstand

after the Detroit Concert Band
in bright white shirts and black pants
under the direction of Leonard Smith
had introduced itself and said it was glad to be there again
and had just been clapped for
and had just started the first Sousa
with a bang and gotten a few bars into it

after the whole neighborhood
had come out as it always did on Tuesday nights
walking over from blocks around—
the old folks, the grown-ups, and the kids—
all waving the mosquitoes away
hearing the gurgling of the drinking fountain
that didn't turn off
laughing and occasionally kicking a bench
in front to the rhythm,
even the grown-up men laughing and affectionate
and shrouded enough by dark to seem
to extend their smiles to me—

and we kids would have gotten up
and marched around the wading pool
if we hadn't been so happy in our front seats on the ground
marching in place,
stepping barefoot on our cool quilts
dancing in the few stars we could see
above the very slowly waving treetops
and streetlights—

until the boys rode through on their bikes
on the path that separated the rows of green benches,
the boys loud and mean and honking and honking their bike horns
and making fun of the music
by imitating it in high-pitched nasty voices—

and the band had to stop and an older man
got up and took off after the boys
and must have caught them
because they didn't come back
and some of the men were saying they'd wring their necks
if they rode through again
and some of the women were wondering about their parents

and Leonard Smith looked annoyed,
looked down the park from the bandstand,
then turned around and crisply
waved his little batons for the band to start again
from the beginning.

I've never been good at understanding
bad. I was bad but didn't know why,
but I knew why those boys were bad—
*bad* equals destroying other people's beauty.
Knowing that, I could never imagine
any of those boys ever being good again.

# Seventy-Eight Mostly Glossy Pictures

of Elvis on my bedroom walls
broke the pattern of the wallpaper
that always drove me nuts
with its ropes on either side
of rows of gray bouquets of roses
making vertical stripes
from floor to ceiling

so when I lay in bed
and looked at the bouquets
my eyes did funny diagonal things
if I wasn't sick
or dizzy already with the flu.

Eleven or twelve bouquets
from floor to ceiling,
and that's how old I was,
and though I used to multiply bouquets
when I was bored,
I don't remember my findings.

I do remember the sum
of Elvis pictures on the walls,
the portraits I sent away for
from ads in *16 Magazine, Teen Beat,
Movie Stars* and *Hep Cats Review,*
and the darker unguarded
newspapery black and whites I clipped
from all the stories in the magazines,
Scotch taping them over redundant roses:

seventy-eight mostly glossy pictures of Elvis,
which would make nineteen on each wall
with two remaining, but with doors and windows
there ended up being two walls with less
and two walls with more—

more of Elvis with his shirt off
reaching for a towel his mother holds
peeking out from a bathroom doorway
with more than his shirt off,
the rest of him just hidden by the door.

Elvis with his shirt off
plopped on a bed in a motel room
tired, dog tired, from all that touring,
the caption reading *TOURING IS THE HARDEST,*

Elvis with his shirt off
arms and broad shoulders
head resting, eyes pensive,
on a pillow waiting with those lips.

Elvis with his eyes
deep sleepy indigo eyes
eyeing me
in vertical, horizontal, and diagonal,
wherever I went in the room.

Elvis with his profile
noble chin and nose and brow,
and lips. Oh, are we back to lips?

More, more of Elvis with his lips
pouting, down turned, softly closed and silent,
yet saying *pleasure*

in the language of lips;
curling, puckered, open, the sly uneven smile,
his bottom lip protruding to be kissed.

Elvis in real life,
hunched over a motorcycle,
speaking on the phone,
petting a dog, tuning a guitar.
Elvis sitting at a piano,
standing against a wall and thinking,
leaning on a fence,
combing his lovely hair.

Hair. Elvis with his hair
neat, slicked back, shiny,
Elvis with his hair disheveled
long warm damp raven.

# Trina

Back before I knew
you could lose a friend
because you talked too much
or had a way of violating
some unknown prohibition

in junior high you walked with me
through neighborhoods in other parishes,
past fortune-teller storefronts in Delray,
past quiet streets where Polish men
stood watering summer lawns,
past southern honky-tonks on Fort Street
where men outside dragged on cigarettes
and made us nervous
when they sized us up.

All over town we walked,
and down by the warehouses and willows
near the darkened river
we discovered the most exquisite stillness
all alone in the city
as the air cooled after midnight.

We rested on rubber swing seats
down at the Boulevard Park,
toeing the dirt and swaying back and forth
without ever swinging

and talked
about everything
no matter how hard or easy—
the boys we liked, the girls at school, the details,
how we thought the world would reveal itself.

Our minds held secrets unknown to us;
we reached for them with words,
and with words we dug them out.

We walked to all the bridges
that spanned the Rouge River
at the limits of the city,
watching them strain to open up
to accommodate the freighters
loaded down with ore
gliding through the passages
in slow deliberate silence
from the bigger river.

We stood with one foot in Detroit
and one in Canada
breathing in the wind
at the center of the Ambassador Bridge.

We walked downtown on one street,
back home on another,
with puddles of black water on the sidewalk
and piles of snow turning into islands,
stood at the corner still talking,
reluctant to part and go home.

We roamed, you too short, too stout,
but with the most beautiful little teeth
that tilted upward when you laughed,
and me, too tall, with kangaroo haunches,
tumbling over gigantic feet,
afraid of all the blood and passion in me,
shocked, sometimes, by my own acute smell.

# Obedience, Duty

*For Trina*


We were good girls who never thought
the Sisters wrong when they assigned us
to the dumb group in ninth grade

where we leaned conspiratorially
a little toward each other's ear,
she taut like a string and me bent like a bow.

I believed in duty
to home and school and church and country.
How I believed in it,

how I believed in the duty to be true.
We figured out the things we'd die for—
loyalty first amongst them.

She grieved about the fire
at Our Lady of the Angels school in Chicago—
she couldn't let it go,

the ninety-two innocents who died
jumping out of high windows
with their backs on fire,

a few asphyxiated at their desks,
their hands steepled in prayer,
their thumbs crossed, their teacher

sitting at her desk facing them,
obediently waiting for the signal
to progress in an orderly way to safety.

Later, after they caught Eichmann
and we knew about the Germans and the Jews,
I couldn't let it go,

I couldn't believe in duty.
I couldn't believe in anything,
until I could affirm survival,

and so we took the bus
to Seven Mile Road near Wyoming
where we peered into the windows

of the Jewish bookstore
to see strange objects,
menorahs and prayer shawls,

and dared to gaze inside—
a handsome young clerk with a yarmulke.
We saw the Magen Davids

displayed on signs
announcing kosher meats and groceries,
so I could try to shake it—

the image of the stars on people's chests
marking them for death,
their death another person's duty.

# I Can't Stop Loving You,

sang Ray Charles
whenever I'd run
out of ice cream
with a full counter
of jocks wanting more
and watching
my every move
up and down
the tunneled stage
of Cunningham's
soda fountain.

So off I'd go
down the filthy stairs
to the basement
to haul up another
of the five-gallon drums.

I could hear the juke
box clearer there
in the semi-dark.
I'd rest a minute,
thrill to Ray,
who sang
for all the men
who would ever
sing to me.

# Georgia Plates

Nobody thought much about it
when he first pulled up,
parked his jalopy in the shade
on the park side
right in front of the lagoon.

One more good old boy
good old car with Georgia plates—
just what you'd expect in the spring of 1956
with all the plants hiring.

Nobody that I knew started keeping track
until the car kept coming back
to the same spot right across the street,
where from our upstairs flat,
and with the car's squared windows,
we could get a real good view.
That's when we noticed the young man
sitting in the driver's seat—

noticed he just sat there,
and noticed that at certain times he got out of the car,
a tall red-faced neatly dressed young Georgia man,
and walked up the street toward Vernor Highway
maybe heading to the bars,
but from the look of him, his mildness,
more likely to one of those joints up there
that featured southern down-home cooking.

And pretty soon we started watching him—
his comings and goings—
how he didn't move the car now,
got out and left in the early morning,
crossed over to the YMCA up the block,
came back with a shave and damp slicked-back hair,

how he sat in the car, left for lunch, came back,
and then left for a long time just before
the changing of the afternoon shift.
After midnight we'd see him back at the car;
he'd crawl into the back seat
and stick his feet out the window facing traffic.

By June we were used to him—
and we felt a little pleased
he'd chosen the spot
right across the street from our house,
clearly the loveliest part of the park.

I'm not sure if it was then we started calling him
Georgia Plates. By this time, some of the men on the block
started chatting with him in the park—*a nice young man*
they said, *up from Georgia,* they said,
but we already knew that,
having seen the Georgia plates.
We figured he'd leave when it got September.

Some Saturday mornings he'd sleep in,
and I worried about those stockinged feet,
with the leaves swirling around the car.
That October it rained a lot,
all those wet red leaves on the windshield,
all our regular habits,
all that changing sky,
all those mice finding shelter,
all those furnaces smelling funny the first time.

When the snow started flying,
he rolled up the back windows.

From our point of view we could only imagine—
he must have pulled those long legs up into a ball;
he might have brought one of granny's feather beds.

One early Saturday morning in December,
after one of those early dripping snows,
I stood at the porch door looking out,
happened to see him pry himself from the back seat,
stand and stretch and stroll into the park.
I knew he was peeing when he turned a little toward a tree,
knew that if I went down to investigate
there'd be one of those yellow holes that dogs make
in the snow. I didn't know what to think about it,
sorting through a lot of things
I just didn't know about—the way men peed
anywhere with ease, and the drunk men
who pissed aggressively in the alley.

The sky is always clear with a million guiding stars
when they let you out of Midnight Mass on Christmas.
On that silent night they shone on him,
sleeping in the car. He was there when we got home.

It wasn't until the middle of March
that one day the car was gone.
Brown frozen leaves ringed a rectangle
of the summer's dry pavement,
and that was all.
For days we waited for him,
wanted him back.
Someone down the block told us they'd
seen his car at a light on Vernor,
but that was days ago.

It was Mama who put the ending on his story—
*I'll bet with all that money he saved*
*he's got enough to go back home*
*and buy a farm.*

# The Time I Took Patsy Walker up to Holy
## Redeemer

to pray for sinners and to sit
in awe in that big Romanesque amber candlelight
of a gray March afternoon in a
one true and only holy apostolic church
with her and her little hillbilly hiccup
and clearing of her throat
        and with her protestant residual
        from her grandmother
            like an Our Father called a Lord's Prayer
            with extra unnecessary words
            and only one other now-I-lay-me-down-to-sleep
                prayer besides
                        like Kool-Aid at that baptist wedding
                        Mama took me to on Fort Street
                        with little stingy sandwiches
                        and bride in a white suit instead
                        of a long-trained gown
                        and *didn't she even have a hat*
                        let alone a veil
                        and it sure didn't last long
                        not much to it

and saw Patsy's big blue protestant child eyes
open wider than my eyes
        because of course I was used to it
        and to hear Mrs. Mulroy
        practicing an Agnus Dei on the organ
        trying to get at some measure
        something on the organ something in the stops

and taught her the sign of the cross
        and she so game, devout, aping me and even
        the ladies there to light candles

dipping their hands into the holy water
on a Saturday afternoon with the weather warming
and it being the third or fourth Saturday in Lent
    I don't remember which
 and all of us knowing the dark time would be coming to an
        end
in alleluia He has risen
        and then Mrs. Mulroy would be pulling out
        all the stops

was the day I knew I was making progress,
        would be storing up some grace in heaven,
        returning one, the first of many I'd return,
            to do my part to amend
            the mess that Martin Luther made
                by not being patient
                    not to mention
                    he later married a nun
                    and it would have to be
                    in a protestant ceremony
                    with God-knows-what refreshments
                    although in those days they didn't
                        have Kool-Aid,

and Patsy had a conversion before my eyes
        like coming home to magic and sure it was
        with all the side altars and the infant
        of Prague in the corner
        along with a pair of crutches on the side
        of Saint Joseph's altar that I'd never seen before
            and didn't see again and wondered about it
            but I could explain it, for it must have been
            a miracle, the lame walking,

and I knew that I could do it myself
    if need be, I didn't need to be a priest to do it:
        *I baptize thee in the name*
        *of the father, son and holy ghost*
if only I had water not grape juice
    or beer or the high-balls that filled so many glasses
    at a catholic wedding
                or protestant could-you-believe-it
                Kool-Aid at a wedding
                cheap and Mama saying,
                *Well you know those baptists*
                *don't drink, but I thought at a*
                *wedding at least*

                but then the wedding was over
                and Mama and I were leaving,
                walking home, and Mama calculating
                the cost of the pillowcases and sheets
            and saying *cheap*, and *the cake was a mix,* and
                *Well, I'm still hungry,*
                so we stopped at that greasy spoon
        on Junction and Fort Street for a nice hamburger,

and I was so glad I was part of the one true and only holy,
    and poor Patsy never even went to church at all
    before I started her on the course to conversion,
    she being my best friend.

# Detroit's 250th Birthday, 1951

In July we ride the bus downtown
to celebrate the birthday of the city—
just Mama and me alone.
Mama tries to be brave;
she must feel lonely in the crowd.
It's our first outing after the funeral.

It's two months after Daddy's funeral
when the float with the birthday cake rolls down
Woodward Avenue with Miss America waving to the crowd.
The rosebud cake looks big enough to feed the city,
but it's made of paper-maché. Brave
among the laughing families, Mama and I stand alone.

Mama talks differently to me now that we are alone.
She started talking that way after the funeral.
Without me as her companion, she can't be brave;
she smiles today, even as we ride downtown,
and tells me how much she loves the city
as we join the others in the swelling crowd.

Mayor Cobo, President Truman speak to the crowd.
They say Detroit is in a class alone.
They tell us other things about the city
I don't understand, grown-up talk, like at the funeral.
Even after dark we stay downtown
and sit on the grass by the river and are brave.

A breeze blows off the straits and we are brave
as we watch the dancers entertain the crowd.
The Empress of Detroit breaks out of a peapod, steps down
from the stage in a gown of sequins to stand alone.
If Daddy wasn't the dead man at the funeral,
he'd enjoy this birthday party for the city.

Daddy said he'd hitched his star to the city.
Mama knows that—that's why she's so brave
joining the celebration soon after the funeral.
Mama explains the costumed people in the crowd—
Cadillac, Chief Pontiac, redcoat soldiers—but I keep names alone:
Daddy worked at Cadillac, owned a Pontiac, drove us downtown.

Cadillac parked his canoe downtown to found the city.
Mama and I are all alone, walking toward the bus, braving
crowds, the summer after Daddy's funeral.

# February Morning, 1952

By the time Mama
throws her clothes on,
wakes me with what I'm to wear,
takes the steps and warms the car,
points it toward the river
and then downriver,

by the time we get there
with her raggedy face over the steering wheel,
my aunts are all gathered,
bickering and starting the reprimands—
Aunt Kay who didn't take her shift,
Mama for living six whole miles away;

by the time the heat of the doorway
hits our cold faces
they are fierce like demons
as they move to claim with stories
the dead one who will be
theirs forever.

My sister is there:
a tall teenager
who will be theirs now,
for she has gone to live
with Aunt Marie,
and she helped with the bathings
of the grandmother
that frightened me—
the white hair on the head,
the brown hair down there—

and my sister was witness
to the six a.m. dying gasp,
and we have only just arrived.

But I am not there.
I am a doll for my mother
to clasp in her grief.
I am a doll for my mother to play with.

Mama gets past the harpies at the door
and falls toward her mother
set up in the dining room
with a white sheet to cover her.
Mama cries like a maniac.
One of the aunts pulls back the sheet
as they all watch Mama.

Mama draws me toward her,
makes me look
at the old woman with her open mouth
and her closed eyes.

She waves me in the face of the dead one
and lets me drop.

# Advanced Cake Baking

From Mama I learned the basics:
to rue and fret over every drop
of batter spilled on the counter
or lobbed up on the wrong side of the bowl.

I learned to sift, measure, resift
three times or more again.
I learned to measure exactly,
pull the knife across the metal cup,
make sure the excess
of whatever is dry and powdery
falls back safely into its container.

I learned to grieve each time a spoon
marked by a prior mixture
was placed on a counter
and not proffered to the new batter in the bowl.
If the Polish lady up the block
used a new-fangled rubber spatula,
with an exaggerated demonstration,
I learned to use a spoon to scrape a spoon.

From Mama I learned well:
feed every drop of the old into the new.
On her good cake days, Mama was delighted,
*It's chemistry,* she'd say.
On the other days
I learned the high agony
of her voice that got into my head
at every step:
*Don't waste.*
*Don't spill.*

Aunt Marie who had no daughters of her own
became the higher secondary teacher.

Her role was to lurk.
When layers came out of the oven lopsided,
she had her fit of wisdom to relay:
*I watched you and I noticed*
*you didn't tap the pans on the counter*
*to tamp the mixture down.*
*That's why your cake is lopsided.*

I learned to tamp.
I learned eventually
to ignore her.

On my good cake days I am delighted:
*It's gravity,* I say.
The oven is lopsided
the floor is lopsided
the house is lopsided
the world is lopsided
lopsided like a family
and the heels of your old shoes.

# Stationary/Stationery

Mama called it the stationary tub,
the cold smooth cement divided rectangle
that stood in the basement,
between the downstairs neighbors'
shiny white-enamel washer with the extra
tub that spun the rinsed clothes
to pull out the excess water
and our old gun-gray 1934 Maytag wringer,

and she used to embarrass me
when I found out the Polish lady up the street
called hers a laundry tub.

Yes, Mama often embarrassed me,
by her age—almost an entire generation older
than anybody else's mother—
by her words that ranged over more territory.

You wouldn't think a fair-minded child
would get embarrassed by her mother's knowledge,
but there it was. It was the 1950s
and that vocabulary of hers
ventured to the verge of uppity.
Besides, the Polish lady up the street
had a brand-new pink front-loading
automatic washer
and a brand-new pink front-loading
automatic dryer to match.
They stood like sly eyes,
one on each side of her laundry tub,
winking and blinking as clothes
tumbled round in them.

And then of course I noticed
when the girl selling flowered sets of writing paper
with matching envelopes rang the bell,
asking if Mama was interested.
The girl showed us three choices, the prettiest
a yellow basket brimming with flowers
at the top right and strewn down the side
with plenty of room to write the news
and mail it off pretty,
so pretty you could imagine
that the person getting it would sniff it,
hoping for a whiff of jonquils.

*Oh, no, sorry Dear,*
*I've got plenty of stationery*
*I never use.*

With Mama around
I couldn't help but learn vocabulary:
we talked of definitions.

Stationary, as in the stationary tub that doesn't move,
that's fixed, that tub I finally got someone
to break up with a sledgehammer
fifty years later so it was no longer stationary—
no longer a tub,

stationary tub that represents a station in the laundry process,
for Mama turning her wringer over the left tub,
wringing the clothes into the first rinse,
turning it over the right tub,
wringing the clothes into the second rinse,
wringing the clothes a third time,
catching them and placing them in the clean basket,
ready to advance to the next station: the clothesline.

Stationery, evolved from bookstores that sold pencils and paper,
stationery, as in the set of pretty yellow-flowered
sheets of paper with matching envelopes that I wanted.

It was only later that I wanted to know:
*Why is it spelled with an* e?

Mama had a fairly good sense
of when she was up against
the whims of the language,
knew when to give up, smiled:

*I don't know. It just is.*

# The Leaders of the Parish

I speak of Holy Redeemer in the old days
and those Irish members of the Saint Alphonsus Guard,
or Knights of Columbus,
or Ancient Order of Hibernians,
or Friendly Sons of Saint Patrick,
or all.

They did good works.
They raised money.
They ran the Wednesday night bingos at the K of C,
the Friday night fish fries during Lent.
At Christmas they hosted the parties for the needy kids.
When they aged, their granddaughters
got to draw the winning tickets
from the huge rolling drum
set up in the balcony of the gym
at the annual Fall Festival
where they always gave away a new Mercury,
bicycles, automatic washers and dryers,
and flocks of Thanksgiving geese and turkeys.

They each wore a little ribbon and a medal
as a boutonnière on Sundays
when they performed their duties
in the Saint Alphonsus Guard
and chivalrously showed the ladies to their seats.
So many of them stood there at the entrances
it didn't matter which door you came in,
you couldn't sneak around them
to avoid the attention.

How important they were,
with their slicked-back hair
their greeting smiles their Irish mugs
right out of Derry, Kildare, Kerry.

How many looks they could give you
when they weren't being ushers on Sunday.
They were full-blooded
and knew their clans and argued about them,
*My grandmother was a McKenna,*
they'd say with ancient pride,
for the name, the affinity, the patrimony
of the clan was there—
far before the serfs had names
far before the English had run out
of place names like *stone* and *brooke,*
run out of occupations like a *clark* or *smith.*

The clan was the thing and they were clannish.
They could look right into you
if they saw you on the street—
their eyes pierced your pale skin and freckled face
and penetrated to the helixes of your genes,
and woe to you if you were found a half-breed,
and even worse, your Irishness
shrouded by an English name.

My red hair piqued their interest:
they gazed as though perhaps they'd seen me
but then on second thought
I didn't exist.

At the bingos and the fish fries
they laughed among themselves
and they were funny,
but if you dared laugh at a joke or even smile
they'd glance quizzically your way
as though a wooden folding chair had sung,
as though a paper tablecloth had spoken.

*What's in a name?* Juliet asks,
and Shakespeare knows: everything.
A name is how you know yourself,
you are Mac son of Call
you are Ó descent of Leary.

# Canvassing in the Neighborhood

Sixty years ago I rang these same doorbells
selling Girl Scout cookies.
And there's no telling which,
if any of them, still work.
I wait. I notice the decay
of caulk, wood, stone, brick;
the repairs done by amateurs
show in the final steps,
the running out of patience—
that splotch of dried paint a memorial
to the end of good intentions.

I gaze through doors and curtains
into hallways and wait.
I knock on rattling aluminum screen doors,
latched, unlatched, it doesn't matter.
I do not open them
to get to the sound old antique oak
of the entry door. I do not want to frighten.
I knock and wait, and yet I know
first stepping on the porch
no one will answer.
Answering the door is no longer
a custom in the neighborhood.

Yet, as always, the neighborhood is more
than it appears and offers surprises;
a ninety-four-year-old man and his wife
invite me to come in,
and I negotiate his English—
talk of his daughter, his gestures,
his wife scrambling, looking for papers—
sure enough, his daughter has taken care
and will collect the absentee ballot.
He tells me, *I'll do anything you say,*

and I notice the glow and thinness of his face,
old enough now to be simplified of male virility.
I know this is the last time
I will see his kind brown eyes.
Along with his vote I receive his blessing.

And then I wait again in the dark porticos of porches
and gaze inside again to see the soundless televisions,
to see the residents turn away from the knocking
toward the flickering.

I smell the dampness
of rotting flyers in porch corners,
remember smells from sixty years ago—
a simmering stew or soup
of a housewife cook,
who ran to the door with wet hands
she was rubbing on an apron.

This afternoon no one is cooking,
just trying to avoid the risk
of being found home.

# Mama in Wonderland

I stand in a pair of pink Bermuda shorts
that Mama bought too big for me
at Lane Bryant where she buys herself
the same white girdles
and the same size 42 white cotton slips,
and when she wears them to ribbons,
she goes back to Lane Bryant
to buy the exact same thing.

The Bermudas are labeled *chubby.*
*They were on sale,* Mama says,
*and, besides, the label won't show.*

We stand in an amusement park
on the Ohio River in Cincinnati.
I'm slightly chubby with big feet,
poised for a growth spurt,
hot and thirsty, sweaty, dirty.
I've gone on the roller coaster seven times,
the Tilt-A-Whirl twice,
then Mama wants to join me on the Ferris wheel
where she likes to see the view.

From the Ferris wheel the sun is setting,
and the Ohio is a sure brown snake
sliding westward.
The road is being widened
to the South, the land of my father;
from the North, the land of my mother;
it bottlenecks at the bridge.
The breeze blows and a few lights shine
along the Kentucky bluffs;
the engine purrs and smells of oil
at the bottom of each revolution.

When we're back on the ground
the breeze is gone. The pink shorts
chafe the new flesh
that swells on the inside of my thighs.

I long to be back at the motel,
but Mama spies a building on the grounds
called *Moonlite Gardens,*
with chandeliers glowing through the open doors.
*Let's go,* I say. *It's hot. I'm thirsty—*
but she leads, remembering something private.

She moves her hoofs with her sensible shoes
that make her feet look even bigger,
enters the ballroom, *oohing* and *aahing*
and doesn't stop until she is looking upward
at the center chandelier, feet spread and planted
in the center of the blond, rosined, maple floor.

The chandeliers are lit; the tables are set in another room,
and the first young women make their entrance
in their ball gowns as she gawks at them,
still *oohing* and *aahing.*
I stand on one chafed leg and then the other,
while they gawk back at us who don't belong.

She gazes and traps me into admiration.
*Aren't they beautiful?* she says too loudly.
*Look at her gown.*
I am afraid Mama will finger the chiffon.

These beauties are not me.
I am a girl who has been given
shorts to grow fatter into.
*Mama, come on,* I say.

*Mama, come on, come on. Let's go—*
but she wants to stay.

I slide along with the snake westward.
I drive all night through Dixie.
I fly eastward upon the wind.

# The Date of the Day in May, 1951

I have endeavored all my life
not to know the date
of that day in May.

I can find it easily enough
on the headstone
if I can just find your grave
somewhere in that section of Holy Sepulcher.

Yet each time I go out there—
only a decade's worth of often—
I get lost pacing
from what I think are landmarks,
treading softly and embarrassed,
prying into other people's dates
of being born and dying.

I know your bones lie there
beside my mother's,
and for that you'd think I'd remember.
After all, I knew her long enough,
even often played the role of mother.

But when you died
I was only six years old
knowing mostly your iron smell
of cigarettes and steel,
the scratch of your weekend whiskers,
your dark-suited height,
your calloused hand holding my hand
on the dates of precious few birthdays.

So I don't know
the date of the day in May,
or when I finally find it

in that row of headstones,
trained as though in theater seats
to look toward a stage that isn't there,
I promptly forget it,

even though I promised my cousin,
your last remaining niece,
that I would get and relay the information.
She wants to fill in the date
in her gilded Tennessee Bible.
She's got her stories of you,
and there's nothing wrong with closure.

But what stories do I have?
I remember no tedium
no drama no gap
no differences of opinion
no teenage rebellion.
With you there can be no end
to a love with only a beginning.
I don't want to know
the date they say you died.

I do remember those Sunday afternoons
I try to forget,
when it was only me and Mama,
the sun beating down
in that treeless section,
disgraced by what was left of our family—
her standing there openly sobbing,
and me standing patiently by,
imagining the other children
at the lakes and on the beaches.

If I could stand her graveside keening
without begging to stay in the car,
she'd stop for ice cream on the way home
at some forgotten dairy on Telegraph Road.

# IV.

## A Time When You Know a House

# On Marking the Fiftieth Anniversary of the Cuban Missile Crisis, or, an Ode on Memory

If I heard the famous speech,
it would have depended
on our rehearsal schedule.

In 1962, October 22nd fell on Monday.
If the president spoke in the evening at eight o'clock,
then *I've Got a Secret, The Rifleman,*
*The Lucy Show,* and *Danny Thomas* were preempted.
If I heard the speech, I know I missed the feeling
that the world would end.

I was a college freshman
just about to find a stupid job working at a dry cleaner,
riding the Livernois bus back and forth to classes,
a history major at the time,
cast as a chorus member in a Greek tragedy

where I learned to trust and sing the praise of memory
that hovers over tapestries we weave
starting with the warp of routine.

I was crazy about a boy who didn't much like me,
hand-painted an "impressionistic" birthday card
of blues and greens that read
*Happy Birthday* on the cover
and then you opened it to *John!*
He didn't much like me
except to neck with me in the stairway
between the space where the theater group claimed our niche
and the debate team hung out on the fourth floor.

John was bound for the fourth floor and law school;
his father had told him to join the debate team,
and all the while I was chasing John
another boy was chasing me.

I was bound for the Players
and the joy of flying up the stairs to get there—
the green room where the cool people hung out—
the repartee, the wit, the first sweet cynicism
of undergraduate intellectuals, the promise
that for the first time I'd fit in.

Now memory scans and picks up threads—
the play, rehearsals, the run in repertory—
and yields surprises in the details:
the opening lines of the play,
the words of Paedagogus to Orestes,
Orestes back in Mycenae and bent on revenge.
*Son of Agamemnon, once general at Troy,*
*now you are here, now you can see it all . . .*
That, and the smell of our coal furnace
once home, the only coal furnace left in the neighborhood,
the October leaves, my sense of freedom, taking late busses,
coming and going whenever I wanted to on my own.

I remember Mama sitting low
in her snagged green frizzy chair opposite the TV—
me bugging her, perhaps,
by perching on the arm of the sofa—
the words of firm and careful measure
from the man I loved and trusted,
the president I would have followed anywhere.
I didn't duck and cover.
I didn't know how close we came.
I remember other things.

# On the Livernois Bus, November 1963

Where did you go—middle-aged woman
on the Livernois bus going southward,
who told me of your husband's suicide
one November afternoon in 1963
the day before I turned nineteen?

I was a sophomore then
going home from classes
when you got on at Puritan,
sat beside me in my favorite window seat,
and rode with me until McGraw
where you got off,
possibly comforted by my rapt attention.

I was not inured to the honor you gave me
as I practiced that day becoming
the woman I was striving hard to be—
generous, gentle, trustworthy, discrete—
a fellow traveler who could sense a tragedy,
listen in a hush without judgment.

I thought about our encounter,
especially since in those days
my mind was fired by will and consciousness,
my own tragedies soon enough
to pass into the recess of childhood
further and further behind me.
I would invent myself as a happy woman
going somewhere,
open to the world with all its sadness.

I thought about our encounter—
beyond Christian charity,
more existential,
beyond self-righteous pity.
For that reason, I never mentioned it to anybody.

It was the silence I loved in me,
and perhaps a little gesture of the body
shifting like a picnic bench
a bicycle, a bus seat,
available to accept a burden.

Silence was important:
after all, a bench or seat
does not smile and tell you:
*that's what I'm here for.*

A week later I rode the same bus
not surprised that the first woman
who got on at Fenkell was crying
while I lowered my eyes
to be discrete,
and then the man at Fullerton
sniffling into a handkerchief.
All the way down,
Plymouth, Joy Road, past St. Cecilia's,
Grand River, Warren, Tireman,
all the way down to the neighborhood,
almost to the river,
the bus filled up with weeping.

Somehow in my self-absorption,
I couldn't intuit
a common cause of grief.
I would walk home

to study for a test in moral philosophy
annoyed at the unusual volume
of the downstairs neighbor's TV,
some frantic male commentator
whose voice I couldn't make out.

Later, after I knew,
after Mama got home,
we stood weeping
in each other's arms.

Where did you go?
I looked for you throughout that bleak winter,
but I never saw you again.
In April I bought the neighbor's car,
rode the bus only rarely after that.

# After the Riot, 1967

A Mercury
so clean—
honest.
You wouldn't believe—
a man and woman
front seat opposite
middle-aged
(she wears a pillbox hat)

drives so slow down Fourteenth
and so wide
you can't get around them
while she points out ruins
and his head stares straight ahead.

It's August now
I never saw the sky so blue at sunset.

# Snapshot Found on the Street Outside the Senate Theater

In the old snapshot
protected by a sleeve
of warn transparent plastic
a GI aims a rifle,
his fingers on the bolt.
He stands ballet-like,
back arched to balance
the weight of the weapon.
He stands on a road
with woods to the right side,
the focus for his aim.
He faces the camera.

He is a young man.
He is a small man.
He has a belligerent half smile.

On the back of the curved snapshot
that seems to have nestled
in a man's wallet
the right top corner chronicles a year,
*1968*, and below is the inscription:
*How do you like the marine?*
*He's strong as an ox.*
*This taken in a combat zone*
*Phu Luc Province.*
*This is where our compound . . .*

The sentence never finishes itself,
and when I find it
at the edge of a snow pile
following a temporary thaw
more than thirty winters later,

the words are still frozen.
And simply because I found it
I have now become connected
to the nameless young man
with the thin-lipped smile.

I look at his face to see
if it will tell me more.
In 1968, the neighborhood was Polish
but that was long ago.
Besides, I don't see it:
no Slavic skull, no deep-eyed oval,
just a pale vaguely southern face,
a face so bare beneath the crew cut
more like my son's
and not unlike my own.

*How do you like the marine?*
he asks and I can only tell him
that standing that way
with the fatigues draping
from his waist,
with the coy left leg extended,
and even with his muscular arm,
I would have thought
he was a graceful girl and not
as strong as an ox.
He wouldn't want to hear that.

We were all graceful in 1968,
the girls dancing in the streets,
the boys sent off to Vietnam.

Through chance I am chosen,
to write the hinge of his story—
whose wallet? Why held so long?
How did it get here?
It is plausible to speak
of an ambush on the road.
It is plausible to kill him off.

It is plausible to supply a father,
the father of the hero,
with memories like eyeglasses
shattered on the snow,
the wrong hands on his loved one,
the father who survived him all these winters
only to lose him again on Michigan Avenue
when he was robbed.

The soldier honors his father.
He speaks of himself in the third person,
speaks like a man, asks for love.

He would be exactly my age by now.

# House

There is a time when you really know a house
when you know
how cold is the cold
water in the faucet
warmed in the wall
and how long warmed water
can spill before the tap starts drawing
the mysterious headstream
from the chilly ground.

You can use it—this knowledge—
to play with this house:
outsmart it as you would a lover.

Wash face hot before the water gets too hot.
Rinse face cold before the water gets too cold.
Husband the water.

These parameters are set for you:
it is within the security of its habits
that you will wink and nod
content to find your freedom
as you move around in it.

# The Big Sister

I.

This must be an early memory.
Mama has put me in a box
to watch her do the wash—
I am in a clean boat
on a coal-glazed basement sea.

After all the loads are wrung and in the basket,
she says, *It's almost time for Betty,*
and takes my box and me
to wait outside.

I am on a sea of fescue grass.
Mama has placed me on the patch of it
that grows along the side yard sidewalk.
She goes in again to get her basket.
She'll come back
to hang the clothes out on the line.

This must be an early memory
because I see my sister dancing home
in a pretty pink and black plaid dress
that seems to be made of grosgrain ribbons.
This is a dress I will later wear.
Her French braids are swinging.
Her dance is called skipping.
She laughs to see me.
She's got a picture she's colored with crayons
that she wants to show Mama.
She can't be more than eight years old.

She is a different Betty than will be,
this one untouched by anger,
grief and jealousy.
I think I am the baby I will always be.


II.


Daddy has stopped and bought Black Jack
on our way back to the car
where it is parked at a meter on Madison.
It is fall, it is afternoon, it is sunny;
we are walking from the downtown library.

Betty and I are Doublemint girls, or Spearmint.
She complains about the Black Jack flavor,
and so I spit it out.
She laughs, they all laugh, when I explain:
*It's too spicy!*


III.


We ride on two-lane roads
that form squares around farmland—
that's the way it was back then.
We are going to the lake,
or maybe Mama's cousin who lived in Maybee.
Early spring, black dirt, plowed furrows, warm day,
the four windows rolled down,
the air fragrant and slightly windy.
Mama drives and sings.
Daddy sits beside her.
I see his freckled arm leaning on the frame.
Betty throws the wrapper from an ice cream drumstick

out the back-seat window.
We turn the corner to another road.
The wrapper blows in again.
They cannot tell in the front seat
why we are laughing so hard.
This is a different family than will be.
This might be the last time I remember
laughing with Betty.

# What Avon Meant to Us

Mama turned my left wrist over,
dabbed Cotillion on the pulse,
dabbed Quaintance on my right.
She made good eye contact,
practicing her spiel.
She was learning
to become an Avon lady.

*Which one do you prefer?*
At six years old I was a perfect subject
with my hands extended
like a little Buddha.

I liked Cotillion,
but later fell in love
with the rosebud cap
on Quaintance.

For Mama, Avon diffused her grief,
and her wish to break sales records
soon got lost in the air of opportunity
to share her widow's plight
with many kind women of the neighborhood.

It wasn't long before her afternoons
were spent at Mexican, Italian,
Lithuanian, and Polish tables,
housewives cooking for husbands
who'd return at four o'clock from day shifts.
The women would thumb
through Avon brochures
looking for specials on hand cream
while Mama ate early samples
of whatever was for dinner.
One time she came home claiming

she'd tried Maltese squid.
Another time it was Alabama okra.

For me, Avon meant color,
arranging the metal sample tubes of lipstick
from Mama's kit in order of preference.
Which did I prefer:
the lightest Plum Pink
or the darkest Blue Flame?

Avon meant a genie of joyful fragrance,
for the minute we slid the battered table knife
under the metal brads that sealed the shipping boxes,
the smell of a thousand flowers
wafted through the dusty rooms.

The boxes came in handy,
for when the doorbell rang, one of us
would scoop the living-room clutter
into an empty Avon box
and cart it off to the junk room
while the other answered the door.

# No More Potatoes

When my children were about ten and eleven I told them
during one of our visits to Mama's dining room table
that from that moment I would not eat another potato—

another potato in any form—mashed, baked, boiled, fried, *au
gratinned,* changed into a chip, put in a pancake. *No,* I pledged,
*from this day forth I shall never eat another potato.*

My children, bred on my humor, saw how absurd the oath,
and, cast as witnesses to my solemn raised palm, played along—
then laughed like crazy, hoisted the specter of holy hell when

a year later I deliberately but nonchalantly
broke my promise. The question that remained is why I offered
such a vow. Because I was still and always taking pleasure

from testing Mama, making sure she was still the same, still there.
From her point of view here was another thing to mull over
in her quiet early-old-age nights. Did she wake up too soon,

before the yellow dawn, and brood, *Why did she say such a thing?
The potatoes were good. The children liked them and ate them all.
Did she say she'd never again eat even one potato?*

How cruel I was to mess with her in her mother's mission
to understand her changeling child who never ceased to challenge,
*I am not you. You are not me.* But I

loved her lovely smile, bemused disbelief before the worry.
Mama had a sense of humor: she could be wry, and witty,
but sincerity, her winning way, demanded that she be

gullible, not to "get it"—flights of absurd silly fancy.
This day she was only cooking, happy to be doing it,
for her younger daughter, mother to her dearest boy and girl,

cooking potatoes for the umpteenth time—not ever a day
she didn't eat at least one potato—in the simplest form:
peeled, poked, cut up, boiled, drained, served hot, with lots of salt
      and butter.

Simple potatoes. She never used that funny mesh basket
someone bought to deep fry potatoes, for the grease would splatter
walls in the tiny unventilated space that passed for a kitchen.

Nor did she ever buy big yellow tins of New Era chips
the Polish lady up the street opened up to vacuum-packed
aroma, tins marked *a healthy food on the alkaline side.*

Ours was not a house that savored French fries or potato chips.
Her potato pot with the handle whose casing turned around
each time you dipped it sideways in sanguine hope of draining it

reminded us that life was not fair, and in this family
we had to learn to outsmart even the metal pots and pans.
That's really why I made the vow, I figure. To stir things up.

# Fallen-Aways

I speak of the young Catholics of the 1960s
who each chose their moment
to defy like Lucifer and say *I will not serve,*

who launched themselves from the orbit of stricture
to come down through the heady atmosphere of the end
of adolescence to catch the breeze of freedom.

I love the way we chucked it all, questioned authority,
laughed at our priest-plagued nun-schooled years
of wringing out our lily-white souls,

obsessively examining them for stains and filthy little sins.
When we ceased to pray to God, we found
some agency inside ourselves to act for peace and justice.

We worked to still our self-hating voices.
We walked in the ways of Zen.
Yet our hearts never really left home.

Our hearts are a cabal of black-robed Jesuit priests
arguing in the night about moral dilemmas,
sly, deft, debating, building airy bridges of logic

to reach the right thing from a common set of principles.
And then our hearts are pedantic little children
proudly reciting lines from the Baltimore Catechism.

We have learned to hide and bear our loneliness.
We sit in rows at funerals, envious of faithful cousins,
who sing heartily, respond promptly, having memorized

nuances of the latest English translations.
We took the rougher road and ended up in the vanguard.
And it is we who most miss the litanies, the Latin.

# Using It Up

When Demery's Department Store went under
Mama got down there just in time
to buy an entire roll of Christmas wrap.
Of course, being Mama,
she didn't get there very fast or early,
and so the patterns left were pretty ugly:
she chose one with busy little mice
in busy little cartoon frames
on a white background. Lots of mice
getting ready for the big day,
hanging up wreaths, decorating trees,
and stuffing stockings.
So many frames of the same cheap thing—
that thirty-six-inch-long bolt
was twenty inches thick.
How she got it home, she didn't say,
All she said was this:
*By the time I got there*
*they were already out of ribbon.*

That was many years ago
and the way I figure,
if I'm generous enough
I have only three or four more years to go
before I use it up—
so I ask the clerks for the bigger boxes
and buy the kids those outsized toys.
Just three or four more years,
and hallelujah, I'll be free. I'll go out
and buy something really nice.

Yet Mama reminds me that her thrift
is far more complicated
than some friend's advice to throw it out,
more complicated than my wish to use it up.

*Waste not, want not,* she always said,
but that wasn't all of it.
There was the added restriction—
to hoard whatever it was you would not waste.
After all, she barely made a dent in it
the fifteen years or so she owned it,
the years she steadily declined.

As I pile the boxes on the table
she's back again, carried in on the light
reflecting off the snow and pouring in
through the big front windows
sifted through the Christmas tree lights.

*If you cut back, it'll see you through.*
*Stop giving so much.*

126

# The Pigeon Nest in the Bathroom, 1992

These were the worst days of the house:
no storm windows, no screens,
me living elsewhere,
death still stinking up the place,
settling in the walls,
the mounds of Mama's junk she left,
and me opening the bathroom window
with the filthy plastic curtain,
raising the only window that would open
and leaving it, forgetting it,
giving the mother pigeon
an opportunity to fly in.

And then later when I closed it
she flew back against the glass
over and over again, bruising the heart
beneath her feathers,
while I hid in the hall
listening to the sound of thumping.

I knew what she felt.
I might as well have cracked her eggs
when I placed the nest in the backyard on the ground
where every squirrel and cat
in the neighborhood could get to them.
It was either that or close the bathroom door,
leave the window open,
leave it to more pigeon splatter on the walls,
more floating little feathers,
the nest exactly centered on the vanity
with its triptych of beveled mirrors.

The worst days of the house:
Christine, my downstairs tenant,
who leaned drunk against my car with growled complaints
or caught me on the front porch steps
each time I'd show up there
working up my nerve to go in.

When I stayed, I woke at 3 a.m.
to the sound of video game gun shots
pinging back and forth,
mortar rounds and anti-aircraft fire
wafting upstairs in a mushroom cloud
from what once had been
a lovely bedroom with high ceilings
and a nice bay window.

I feared the joists, the floorboards,
the old substantial ceiling plaster
were all giving way
and what was lost was privacy.

And then the pigeons.
Mother Pigeon with your wanton ways:
I shut you out.

# Upon Falling into Blue Heron Lagoon Two Weeks
## Before My Seventieth Birthday

*Belle Isle Park, Detroit*

Maneuvering at water's edge
the final post of a chain-link fence
that separates the wilds from a golf course—
I grabbed a branch on the bank for balance
as I swung around. It gave,

and I floated down to the water
in a whorl of yellow leaves
with the distant sound of traffic
in the bright November sunshine.
I immediately started to laugh.

Falling backward, my body folded forward;
and butt first, I felt the down coat's feathers
forming lumps like in an ancient pillow
I remember as a child—
like bouncing on a bed, like landing on a cloud;

and though most of my body was soaked,
my heart and head were dry
along with one good arm.
How easy it was when I finally scrambled out:
my shoes were squeaking, but I wasn't cold.

I noticed something new: water that looks cold
doesn't have to be;
water spun through lakes and straits
to fan out shallow in an isle lagoon
can hold the memory of summer's effervescence.

And now it must mean, must signify something—
this floating fall, this soft dunk of water.
And so I mull it over, ponder:
am I born again or blessed, and to what purpose?
Though first of all I must confess:

I've lost my faith in easy signs,
and my range of speculation narrows.
I may be *losing all my highs and lows*
like the Eagles' "Desperado";
if feeling goes away, then nothing means nor matters.

Yet I know my feelings haven't *gone away;*
I'm only lulled by lovely lyrics set to mournful tunes.
I feel, therefore, I am, though I must work with who I am.
My *soul* must *clap its hands and sing, and louder sing,*
says the poet Yeats, *for every tatter in its mortal dress.*

Could that be the septuagenarian's skill
that I'm awaiting? My soul to clap its hands and sing?
To sing of places that I love from knowing them,
through years of knowing them, to fancy myself
an oracle of knowing them—now and way back when

when we skated across lagoons and under bridges
to the mouth of the canal, where only a spit of sand
stood between canal and river: red sun, circle of slush,
end of ice, dark pool—wind that cuts through earmuffs
to have its way with summer's effervescence.

# Down by the Boulevard Dock, 1977

*A Poem for the Detroit River*


Whitman could not have sung you justice
nor can I
river misnamed a river
more a braid
of ocean lakes
weaving gray ribbons and releasing them
into Erie's dark conformity

where old Black ladies
and my old white mama
fish off the dock
and never catch anything,
but ask each other
*Catching anything?*

and watch the cast of water currents
and paper cups tell destiny
and are comforted—
old age the knot that ties the braid.

Down here at the foot of the Boulevard
I gaze against the wind upriver:
the bridge to Canada and freedom—
the skyscrapers against afternoon sun—
I rejoice in them and Coke spills on the concrete,
the cans, bottles, glass, permanent
concrete benches, aimed toward insight—
the river shall make us love
the course of our folly.

I see the dock
backwards in my experience
my father's hand to hold me back
before the concrete was poured,

brown cedar pylons sunk in the current;
a big boy jumps from the shore
and scales one;
we are open mouthed—
certain death undertow—
my father's hand grasps tighter;

and other times the lights at night—
the sign on the bridge burns
*Ambassador*
and I neck with a boy
in a parked car—
white streetlights,
the intermittent breeze,
the smell of water,
the sound of lapping.

Now I hold the children's hands tightly—
the boy must go too near the water
drags me shivering
to where the concrete drops
*What is an undertow?*
wiggling the toes in his sandals

and so I pull him back to sit
on the bench where we lick Good Humors;
the freighters drag heavy
the mail boat rides high,
while the girl, silent and full of oceans
and fish that won't be caught,
tells us of her plan
to invent a river cleaner.

The wind picks up at sundown.
Fishermen retreat,
the lovers are due,
odd children, mine among them,
connected to fishermen and lovers,
run through indestructible turf
growing over homogenized ruins
of a warehouse;
the old john built like a temple
from the turn of the century
stands but is padlocked
and the drinking fountain
fails to work.

# Thanks

The Detroit area offers a supportive community for poets, and many of my Detroit poems have been revised and made better over the years after sharing them in master-level poetry workshops—first under the auspices of the Writer's Voice of the YMCA, and then under the auspices of Springfed Arts. Workshop leaders I wish to thank include: Linda Nemec Foster, Alvin Aubert, Mary Jo Firth Gillett, Lucinda Sabino, Kristine Uyeda, Diane DeCillis, Dawn McDuffie, and Kelly Fordon. Fellow poets who wove themselves in and out of these workshops are all to be thanked, even if too numerous to mention.

I thank Ann Russell for a suggestion she made while reading an early draft of my prose memoir, *The Way-Back Room: A Memoir of a Detroit Childhood* (Published by Bottom Dog Press in 2011). I had placed a few poems between chapters, and though related, they did not advance the story. "If you take them out," Ann said, "you can collect them for another book."

I thank Diane DeCillis and Christine Uyeda, who at different times read parts of the manuscript and offered encouragement when it was in the doldrums.

I thank Gerry LaFemina, who in 2013 suggested a viable arrangement of the poems. I thank Russell Thorburn for doing the same thing in 2019 from a considerably expanded version. Russ also helped me find the real title for my book, after I'd worked with what I'd thought was a "good-enough" title for years. It made a lot of difference.

I thank Nancy Owen Nelson for encouragement and leads on the publishing biz.

I want to particularly thank Anne Doran who read the entire manuscript in the summer of 2019 and commented on almost every single poem. Her attention inspired me to look at many of them with a fresh eye.

I thank Ama Carey-Barr, Diane Dickinson, and Mary Schmitt, who along with Anne Doran and myself, form the poetry support group we call the G5. I thank the G5 for sharing their poems, for responding to mine, and for becoming the daily study group that is getting (got) us through a pandemic. All-for-one and one-for-all.

I thank Jen Anderson, my copy editor, who was a delight to work with. I thank Dwight Stackhouse for his lovely photographs. I thank Shay Culligan at Kelsay Books for the layout, and Karen Kelsay for providing a publishing home.

I thank the real people in my poems for being (having been) so endearing.

# About the Author

Mary Minock grew up in the 1950s and 1960s in the dense Southwest Detroit parish of Holy Redeemer during a time of remarkable changes. Eventually, she left Detroit and went on to live in a series of college towns and New York City. She moved back to Detroit in 1996, fixed up her childhood home, lived there for more than a decade, and then moved three blocks away to help restore another stately Detroit home where she resides today.

She is the author of *The Way-Back Room: A Memoir of a Detroit Childhood* (Bottom Dog Press, 2011) and a first book of poetry, *Love in the Upstairs Flat* (Mellen, 1995). She has won several awards for her poetry, including an Allen Ginsberg Poetry Award. She is a three-time winner of the Gwendolyn Brooks Award for Poetry from the Society for the Study of Midwestern Literature.

Mary has recently retired as professor emerita from Madonna University. Before that, she taught at Wayne State University, New York Institute of Technology, and the University of Michigan.

www.ingramcontent.com/pod-product-compliance
Lightning Source LLC
Chambersburg PA
CBHW070332090426
42733CB00012B/2455